AMLETHUS
BOOK I

BY
CARL MELANSON

First Edition

Biographical Publishing Company
Prospect, Connecticut

AMLETHUS
Book I
First Edition

Published by:
Biographical Publishing Company
95 Sycamore Drive
Prospect, CT 06712-1493
Phone: 203-758-3661   Fax: 253-793-2618
e-mail: biopub@aol.com

All rights reserved. No part of this book may be reproduced or transmitted in any form or by any means, electronic or mechanical, including photocopying, recording, or by any information storage or retrieval system without the written permission of the author, except for the inclusion of brief quotations in a review.

Copyright © 2012 Carl Melanson
First Printing 2012
PRINTED IN THE UNITED STATES OF AMERICA

Publisher's Cataloging-in-Publication Data

Melanson, Carl.
Amlethus: Book I/ by Carl Melanson.
1st ed.
p. cm.
ISBN 1929882777 (alk. Paper)
13-Digit ISBN 9781929882779
1. Title. 2. Christianity. 3. Jesus Christ. 4. Shakespeare.
Dewey Decimal Classifications: 230 Christian theology;
810 Canadian literature in English
BISAC Subjects: REL070000 RELIGION / Christianity
REL067000 RELIGION / Theology
LCO006000 LITERARY COLLECTIONS / Canadian
Library of Congress Control Number: 2012918797

Book I

Every rose must die, and its beauty must subsist; but it cannot be love, nor loss, for whose exegesis the gardener grows himself an ethic by whose ghosts I dither in the dark. It nips it in the bud, but if truth takes out the past from the augur's mind, it becomes a leaf whose atavism's in the tryst of constellations. Perception's a disciple, truth is an unknown messenger. This grave I dredge accosts my mind with arcane foresights of paradise and hellfire intermixed. O the sartorial web, truth's churlish prelacy's in a huff; the Universe is troubled by foolish twilights; it aspirates our conviction that time's incognito, like the philosopher's stone, wherein false solicitude deepens with falser gen to make an alibi with the poet's idiom, broken like a mirror to the context. Ponder it then, for we do not know how to bring our demons to damnation without ethereal and wraithlike excuses. It's the art of losing oneself, an established sense of irony that one does not live twice. Love endures all profligacy, and does not create it. I sleep in God's hostelry, though I question the hotelier's omniscience. It revises my clout with lewder sympathy than death in a dreamless crowd. Who armours time and calls it duff in panoply; who strikes the hardest end of ration until his wisdom breaks? O mete the mind of God to Infinity, for much moves in language that spiders will not sense, therefore fear not the consequence that nature cannot further grot. O that fire could predict its own delusion, that it could be the omen to its own purpose, how then would time tremble when his fear is as far ahead of itself as a boatman in a desert? O stars of Galahad, be then the features of an infinite mind in search of itself. A seer troubled by the twilight of the gods and various idols in the heavens. In these orbs of fire I am reborn like Prometheus. Who holds so fair an omen to winter's mind that fire comes quick in brainstorms when it knows the pith is slow. O my brains . . . vestiges not so moot as to settle fire's questions about the Sun. Truth is not what we must seek, but what we should notice is real when realness is not what compares to what, but mere comparison when both injunctions rue at the tremor of a butterfly. Return, Apollo, to whatever mind divines you; in which duplicity's the only allure, like a fish whose regency culls the fisherman's demur. He is returned to childhood visions, chiaroscuros in mind forever and ever. O Will of the world, come you here to reveal me to myself like a madman to his own mirror? With increase of knowledge comes increase of sorrow. O apocryphal poesy of the age, men seeking intuit where none is hidden. To your mellow end, good fellow; a beggar, lying doggo in's grave, but who will give his bones to a ballyhoo; who will nurse his brain like a galoot in a treasury, or a gumshoe in an unmysterious room? Am I not much wiser than my mistakes were long ago, though the rain bird alerts me of no pilgrimage of choice to tear my raglans over without any previous existence? I beg you for another look into the mystery, where discovery pewits over the strangeness of your wonder. But dreams satirize the mind and the soul, they make me pensive as a playwright's retort, unbridled to the maxim minds must fledge to understand the flightiest flight. Tender yet the chrysalis of uncertain vows, the mind syncopates and mulls over its own symphony, and is left to shun its outworn self-séance—like a cordage of words; forgotten like a book in a sheathe of snow, its tales now bounded in imagined circumstances. The poet, like a vampire drowned in blood, looks at life like a trestle that he himself cannot cross since he is crass. O let me escape tradition awhile, though it's the predecessor to all knowable nous, the onus of my mind . . . a gambler to certainty, a predictor of the past! Like a poet sapping his inspired spirits, sipping on absinthe, awaiting the green sprite of inspiration, poems read us with more kismet than a rhymester at a politician's grave, or a shrike in this the most solemn pour of our lives. The scanty deference never emerged so acutely, like a man happily forgetting the concertos of war within himself. This is why the age responds to us like demons in a barn, when genius begs a fairy for her guiles and leaves her to testify the truth: it absolves what is timeless and puts the dead to rest, in the remembrance of these timely scops. Let us remember the poems, for though we shan't recite the equivalence of our Saviour, Jesus, none shall grow among the lilies of a parable unless they grow to seed, like lepers seeking the cure within the lazar's blood. Surely erstwhile ways should bequeath us a stranger's many minds. After all, who caroms the plot with more dimensions than science has ever dreamed? Do not say these phrases are lame, for someday they shall walk like Lazarus out of the grave. I'll edify them like tribes in use of useless passions; I'll dispel the stratus of their minds and rain upon their wonder like an ancient mystery. One should never remain the set phrase within himself; nor adapt to what he has mistaken as his life, like an embryo with consciousness enough to overtake the surrogate mother, instead of lunging at what death will take from him, for a stone is a stone forever, but a man is never twice a moment; a man is at once the dream and the dreamer, the witness and the incident, he is the very disaster which he dares upon himself with closed eyes. He would heal a thymus to such a blue moon that I scarce could speak without my thankful equipoise to God. If that ogre, Death, comes to malinger my spirit, my mind's not booted to the climax of the paragon; it plummets to graver things than this, like labour, thinking, love—O cruellest Moloch of Passion! You must not fear it. Awareness is a light unto what we do not know. I weep when the auger's will coddles the earth, as though Plato were the chine wherein parodies rankle for the laughter of gravediggers. The ghosts of poetry swagger in the light, and plunge into the chorus of angels and make them dread the instance when they will lose the light by desiring it. Leaves of Grass grows to seed . . . the book's argot is indecisive, the words trending mostly by the easiest passage. The codger's gander will not surcease the gamut, nor pry honesty from Lucifer's nub. Would we refuse the words of a Messiah, if in them we found our truest selves? O that I could eat more succulent prose than Baudelaire's obsession with melancholy. The mystery will suffer itself like a lonely old man at a bazaar who ponders his purpose beneath a sickly cloud. Now to repose where God tends to my most beautiful dreams; my sickness is no longer binary by the gin it is caught by! Then let Nature dwell in your mind, and let that be your imagination; let the Universe dwell within you, and let that be your consciousness—the sacred heart hags on our longings, like an old diversifier in the kindling. Backward we may think, forward we may discover—in this peculiar light, I am become a No-man. O this eidolon warns me sincerely. The Draconians slander my furore, fill my poll with self-doubt, and claim I have been bettered by my state of undress. Ha! They are the mystery that regrets the intrigue, the clue that doubts the assertion, a man standing in a weakening ray of light who yet believes it cannot wilt and die away. They've proven their patience to be feebler than a surd, when he tergiversates his will to become the solution. Silent, like the layabout's maiden when she must moil in muftis's cell, they would be gutted by the rotes, like a fish that cannot stand the brine, if only they knew my knowledge. O poets! A murder of crows who crow about heaven unpronounced of any guilt! Apollo's Apocalypse throws illegible ghosts into the mist, our farthing minds to the better clouds of Elysium. It's in this era that the neophytes will return from the firmament of Pleiades; long awaited from the simpleton prophecies that held them to their drab slavery, to believe in the limits of the Infinite Mind! There is a stairway in each of us, in which a satirical despot devours our intrigue, whose transcendence justifies our descent into the abyss. In shufties of beauty there are gazes of madness, like seconds that peek into eternity and create its backlash on the moment to return to itself as a memory. It suborns in us all the qualities of our sufferance that we peek into very our souls and find that the stairway, not its descent, is the enemy. You see the dead with the sagacity of a ghost in a war too bloody for the General's gape. How general is your sickness that it holds an audience to its pogroms and sends them through to the other side of the looking-glass? This man's entopic mouth should be stuffed with echolalia like a paladin in an olden souk of clichés. Aye, seems like a shyster to me. To you, it may gobbledygook; to a fly it could be a hoatching of dead flesh, in which its kin births itself under death's proviso. Would you eat an omen like an urchin and tell me the prophecy is not what starved you to begin with? Love's a great preamble for a literati such as this. Ay, those people, those swindlers of heart-and-soul whom you call brothers, sisters, friends, neighbours—ay, they . . . they would steal a lazar's soupçon and maculate the leper they claim to heal. O Son of Man, forget that fib, there is no truth to be discovered in it; the trough of his mind is within a Confucian kind of confusion, which he creates in those who dispraise him; it is his victory, like an autocrat on a plinth—mine is more within the laboriousness of it all. Truth's trove is the philosopher's impediment, since philosophy is but the shadow of truth, and truth must be without shadow to be tacit and understood. Our souls' tropology, like an invisible troubadour, is the focus of our minds, since our tropic tears would drown our desert's ode to God's subpoena. Ay, the dirge is done; do not shilly-shally like a shadow in the night. Guess it as you may, it's equally a trouble to your spirit. To me the words are like a blind man's reprisal—ay, the settling of scores—to me they are as fusty as a truffle of dirt. What so far you have sought in the bread of life is exactly what you have missed in the dearth—that you are within my industry when acumen concerns you, and the scullion enslaves you in the plover's hearse. You must be cruel to speak the truth. I'll drop the eaves even on he who beguiles me to my repartee! Bosh! I guttle it like a toad devouring a toadstool. Does it spill the feelings into the right beaker; or does the cup spill its troubles to the floor for everyone to see? We seek what is tangible, but is it tangible to seek? Don't be a prem to the pedantry's mechanism, if the birth is the cause of your suffering; for then the mechanism perishes in your Pooterish disclaim. Two perfect players would go on playing forever. The art of a mime is not in what he performs, nor a painter in what he paints, nor a poet in what he compiles—it is in what it makes us feel. Do not dare feel these words, if you have not touched their meaning. Reality misunderstands us all sometimes. Who can hear the truth beyond the grave of a quant, a madman? Do you detest it, abhor it? I abhor its outset on man's liberties. We exist where existence is dispirited, a trifle where opposition wreaks its compliance to heckle our anguish like a comedian on a rostrum or Hamlet on a dais. We think ourselves wise, yet such a thing requires us to mull over the details, for in ponder we escape existence to swot it up—it nonpluses and flummoxes us all merely because our thoughts play their part by guessing what we are. I'll baptize you a pretender for now, and your twinges will despond their recreation in the epic of a kip, for reality is the dream you'll never understand. I'll squire you to a rood, and wassail at your tomb like a broken-hearted apostles. *"O God, forgive them, they know not what they are doing."* Does He induce His love with the method of a shadow to make us fear the Sun? Politics' asters in the clouds! There is no mystery in the sea when the outlook renders us its insight, and mechanisms relinquish the defence we force them to exert—should you force a lion to eat his quarry? The animal who digs himself a refuge doffs the predator's comprehension; what darkness must we endure to compare it to the shadow of He who seeks to hybridize the mystery of a cloak with a ghost's predation on reality, where we dig ourselves into oblivion to practice abandon? Must we relate every tear to he who is as remorseless as a brigand at a play, who eyes the scene with dumber scold than a beggar panhandling beggars more skint than he himself? It's a false dulcet to the ear. Ay, they ratiocinate my temper, my sulk, my strop, my fit of pique—their semi-setose faces should be repudiated by this. Am I the fetlock of their outrageous cram? I provide no stench to roses by smelling them, so why do they, in this symposium make me wear a crown of thorns, and seek to sniff out my synoptic aroma like a thyme? They judge me; but their judgment is stranger than anything a man can do. They say I am barmy and that I round the bend, one in the melodrama of his own fantasies. Then to you, as to I, they whoop it up with their own sway, though it vies against them too! They think life is a concubine in a masquerade . . . she must be weary of her veil to be so obviously sad. Self-hatred is to recognize one's demons in another man; when they entertain us with their vanities and gainsays, we begin to fear ourselves like self-conscious ghosts. My lungs are full of music then; but are your ears plentiful enough to treat them as common to your knack? Ay, I think it does its work—it is not yet in the clouds but it comes, it comes. But they, those brigands of the mind, they have nothing in them but false gumption . . . they play hide-and-seek with God and claim to find nothingness. They rag on my ethics as though the truth could not bleed without their procedures. They miscue their ambitions if they deem my grounds to be stranger than theirs. It's their sole interest to make themselves meditate after they interpret my pedestrian flight—they cannot pebble my pebbledash, nor may they assume that I am their outlier's penologist. Ay, they ponce about, compressive of my impulse and in doing so exemplify their own, and think themselves concealers of the chameleon. How dare they be the broncobusters of a steed who is already temperate. But, this is the truth, Solomon, while I swim in ataraxic pools, they drown in oceans they cannot comprehend. Let me enounce the duke-the-beetle's phase: first he questions, then he realizes, then he distorts the common frangipani of truth to elicit the gambit of a breath. When I tap upon an empty jar, water mourns the echo of existence; when I tap upon a gondolier's skull, it's the goner's hope that something fills it with more of a nub than water, for such a thing would seem a madman's delusions—a falseness I cannot transmute without dragging you into my very grave. The jackal's requiem would swindle your art of its essential application, and expend your convictions like pilliwinks on a snake—such punishment is a self-enraptured circus. Don't prize the scruple of a clue and tell me the sleuth's intelligence is less conquerable than a beetle in the bog. They say that I am mad, frenetic to the bone, but don't let yourself be foozled by these judgments, for they are vultures unto themselves and each other: madness is only that trait of mind when one has figured out too many of God's secrets, even while he cannot demarcate them, nor meet their Maker. It mugs up your consciousness like an empty tarn, which is not outside the echo of heat when the fire's gone; it is more solemn to the blood, more invective to native silences. The poet must seclude the talking ghosts of the past, the present, and the future, to their own interim; Dante's divinity shakes the evolution of the stars. It is the dour exception to mirror it in the poet's mind, and become the muscled hint that clutches to the mystery—does the mood create the dance or does the dance create the mood? Ay, the patient etherized upon the table is quickly drying up. Literature is dying like an old man weary of his own sleight of hand; pluck out the ear of that particular madness and speak to it, that you might know what the madness is all about. You will overhear less sense than a scamp at a Chaplin-flick, or a mischief maker at a do. But since you are a poet, and I teach not blindness how to settle for its groping; here in Amlethus madmen are the common capon, eccentrics flock to the market for natters about the mind, in good spirits for their insolence. You must mount up your forte more readily. The atmosphere must be willing to provide lodgings for such a mind if it is to do its work. I beseech you to consider where these roads may lead compared to the ones that have taken you where you are. Speak the queries of a bell, but let not the toll destroy the ivory tower . . . my puerile mind is but a trifle, it has become but a coddled brain in the aplomb of wit and wisdom, the thespian ghouls of time suffer the drama of backward augury. I remit the world within my memory, where I brew my gripes about times now forsaken as a whole, in whose dungeon deceptions swarm and plunge into its abyss like suicide romantics. Ay, my return to forgotten lands, where fire turns Precambrian sands to glass, has made me into a rambunctious thinker yet a more normative man. O how it connives against me . . . to know that the convivial intelligence of love outthinks my teetotaller's warren, to whose course I owe my thoughts, yet to none do I owe my life. My tears insist on a soul-aimed cadger, for it's therewith that thoughts are born to envy the timeless mind of Hamlet. Am I a fool? Am I a madman? When duplicity lashes at the credence of a book, it cannot sustain the metaphors within itself, for time's red herring gins the animal it sought to ensile for eternity forevermore. Our inquiries solemnize our answers into the art of regret; for our discoveries are now cacuminal, and we lose ourselves within lands wherein we are outsiders. But, pixilated by these occasions, what flounders our thoughts is the ignominy of action; what halts our iniquity appeals to the accouterments of fear, whose ad-libbed theatrics make mouths at the invisible event like Hamlet's quandary. But when resolve hinders our passions, to egg in us unhatched plots, truth discovers our most abysmal adages, whose bridges are words that meet the ends of opposites, to transmogrify them into chameleons of each other. It's a veritable gallimaufry in the keenest sense of the word. We are helots, serfs of consequence; we pay our debts with greater debt, and dig the gravedigger's grave to become what we swore never to become—the very thing that warrants our dirt as a secret more horrid than what we bury. We're all insane with diverse ideas about insanity. I desire to be no one, yet in my desire, am an Everyman and a Noman all at once . . . Such things are paltry, since faith's barter for denial can combust but a flame in a candelabra. The mind of God is a self-reference to its own mindfulness; the Buddha's secret enlightenment—all such triumphs rescind themselves like two armies with tantamount ascendancy. When desire desires us, it suffers our absence as we do its presence. To be against anything is to feed the innards of the lion you seek to starve. Eden was lost, for if God's law had not become their hair shirt, their sackcloth, what apple would not have been consumed? The Tree of Knowledge would have died because of them. Desire is hell; the temptation of Eden was not the tree, nor the apple, but the temptation itself. Forsake desire's littlest iota, and suddenly you behold the Universe in your hand. Why should you seek something you have not lost? Looking for God is to lose Him in the sway, it's like bringing up the rear in a stranger's house. Onlookers cannot see the truth, for, in looking, they lose what was already theirs. Return to Eden, but do not look for the way, for that is where you are currently lost, which may once have been an empire too bold for its own exigency. A misanthrope's potentate repels the simplicity of this act, whose rigmaroles scourge stupidity to teach it its own method. Don't be he who suffers for nothing, until something fulfills him; be he who's fulfilled before fulfillment is ever to be had. Such is the secret of enlightenment. You are not the life you are currently defining; you are not the words you think, the pains you feel, the virtues you choose, the poetics you succour, the points you make, the visions you engross—you are the blankness of them all. A frogspawn is born with blankness and begins to observe, to feel, to think, deceiving itself with the fabrics of the Universe. How to keep the blankness? The blankness is the entire mind, while words, ideas, feelings, imagery, memories, these are merely the components. Meditate on the blankness, and all sorrows, heartaches, identities, philosophies, will disappear and let you be yourself. Let the words do discourse with your soul; ay, your very mainstay. A man cannot be lost at sea if he understands the workings of the stars, nor can he grumble in himself if he understands his own mind. Alas, you've become the shriver's gizmo—your silence is the folklore of your contrition. Do not marvel at my humble Hogan, nor at anything that your soul may fool you into commiserating; if you are to survive a nuclear winter like a Croton bug. The dead cannot have ambition. Let death honcho your life—let it oppress your will. The grackle's whinge shall substitute your silence, and gradate your fear to seek the echelon of your brain. Ay, the keeper's take; the taker's leave; the leaver's muse; the muser's talk; the talker's prowl; the prowler's potential; the potentate's love; the lover's doom; the doomsayer's keep—O but I must beseech his mind to carouse in my work; it's Malpomene's regret. You shall not find it. Now go your way, and catch a fish before it catches you. The pilgrim does not need the journey to exist, it's the other way around. O Solomon, it is not at all a calaboose to your wisdom. Verily, I say unto you: I seek nothing, and in that nothingness find everything I need. These words are but the sails of a lost man, empyrean to his own conceit. Tell me if its power is more eloquent than anything I've conjured from his own Santeria with Satan. He yokes my memory like a hook in oil . . . Death indeed is the mystery that frights us the most, and yet, though our looks are horrid to host its imperial Eye, we do not shy away from such a vision as we would any other fear. I'll read it with greater inquiry than Herod on Cleopatra; an inevitable reader, a pulpit who swots his more difficult conjuror, whose spells no eel debunks as wires to its head. O I am such a skell to bribe myself with these stages; yet skulk to none, I am better than a liar. With a mere browse I am wanton to misjudge it.

In it, beauty parted from me, my heart estranged by its forage. It shows prowess beyond the capacity of a man, though a skeleton wouldn't flicker in's grave to know the feeling's dead. Are you too keen to be rational or too rational to bolt the entremets, the piquant viands, that await you in the grave? Are these words as emetic as her fare, her repast, or is there more ration in us than their cogitations avow? Do you palisade your speech so well that it writes its words upon your wall? Does the palimpsest of my heart overwrite what once was spoken of my spirit? Your mind pettifogs in its own trials of dust—the storm dies down with equal reverence to its birth. I must be a diviner, you're like a dryad in the Sun. It's what elides my heart but the jonquil's inquest cannot reason with the shell's averment, and so festers in the metaphor. Are you as thalassic a theatre-goer as a fish who cannot swim? Swot yourself like an oppressor in a cage, for complicity cannot stomach the vengeful mollusc of habitude. Ay, but tyrants still have known the lie that eases itself into the natural blood of a lion, not before his sovereignties are assured their seating in the plenums of arguable histories, lest war becomes his temperance, and temperance his prideful stake in the honest man's diversion. O how it booties me of my happy joy, to crow about that polyglot crusader's triumph, when, hacking the gumption from my literature's provender to feed it to the keen, I hinge the crux of my mind with the modern bookworm's indolence to open up the deepest pangs of my conscience. With the increase of solemn blether deeply stowed in the carper's heart, what accouters my sensation with the scullion's goose-bumps, when he must swallow words already served, is as a bulwark of defeat. The pressures of headship in these literary squabbles, like an executioner who must trudge to his daily spot of bloody death, seems my lackadaisical tariff, and I shudder at its rubric activity within the ruing of my brain. For I, in my own shadow's sophistry, must sop myself in darkness to understand why the sunlight seeks me to be damned. Since your art seems to cause men their brains' duricrust, like a Palaeolithic desert mirage, then why not precipitate the dream, that the prodrome of our soulful reverie might not rigout our cerebral vagary? Go to Lucifer for your tang of language; mine's tart at the moment—it bites at none of the edge he's akin to. Apollo's butterflies are at vigil in my stomach—but, mark me, he's not a poet by matter, but by attire—a Marlovian fluke with a fleece more fantastic than what it covers. My barb and spike have been at war with themselves since my last attempt to oust him as the ghost in the machine. Like a fearful old lag, I rib the rub, and deny that its victuals sleep in my house, as though sense could no longer teach itself so common. Would the tattie-bogle fear the crows it seeks to deceive? Simplify your trade or else the tradesmen will flout you out the door. The spalpeen is in your heart and the haboob is in your skull. You jalouse my footling doom, if I skive my complacency. Is this the resolution of passionate men—to shut themselves away and be riddled by their fears 'til doomsday? If it be so, then the oscitancy of my spirit is also my dear love's lassitude. There remains a baseless fear in passion's apex, that I am become such a ghost whose drabness haunts no one, whose presage cannot absolve a crowd beyond what they themselves negate. Ay, it's those who, with intellectual armours, aggrandize their shallow quintessence like a quisling's unction, from whose apostasy they would appropriate their most devout religious cause. For like his brain's arroyo, his passion is in arrears with death. Alas, to force accretion in the soil of afflatus, so that all might see that there is a rose's pod in every man's odious head. Ay, love is quite saccharine to inspire madness in the greatest men. Your self-made macrocosm is fleshed like a heart in a cufflink. Why I have such a mind I cannot say, for poets, clamant in their continuum shells, are the most self-indulgent creatures in all of Eden. I could concretize the curios of night as though they were less inspiring than an ancient fossils, and yet I cannot make the egger's effusion seem boggy to Egyptian souls, who thirst to see me swallowed by the eagle's eggshell or the butterfly's cocoon into ancient methods of expression that even Homer would send back to the witch that cursed him. Have we not yet surpassed the politics of the Romans? So why do we recap the labour of our poets with phrases that keep trying to die? It's in my blood . . . it's my nature—proud men may pray within their own whitewash hearts, though their dogma advocates self-sympathy. The lion's den, though it promotes the animal's carnal force, also makes him the victim of his nature. Can you make fire an element not requisite of a star? Ay, there's a theatre in my brain, wherein ne'er-do-wells gather together to prang my charades, though theirs are likewise conscious of the scene. It's like glaucoma's fray on the poet's sight, who recites his glops of flannel, his jaw to the crowd; ears whose tenants, like armyworms' arrant navigations through unsettled fields of dust, hear the words but know not the artillery within their literary canon. Ay, what makes my thoughts so prim, so heathen to their cause, is that of truth made raw-boned by art's very glut. As theatres must suffer to retain their conscience, such pinpricks must retain their chancy grub, like the teredo's role in the ship of time, lest our very thoughts become heathen to our brains. What am I? A sleuth to truth and beauty? Who is it that knows nothing yet speaks all his knowledge in a caprice? Who is it that disperses his doubt as wisdom, his stenches as fragrances, his conceit as a nap, raising his privations to the teeth? Cover it like a clown whose circus scuppers his exuberance of spirit with the measly prowess of his passion. Such a man, by the bickering of his cosseted brain, would solder his bore to his very skull. There's a strangeness in such a man that sometimes snags his humble manners to the judgment of hooligans and hawkers; yet to speak of provender to he who feigns the hunger is a method too often considered in the mind's wastelands to sprout a ration there. For fevers would neglect their own dotage if it brought them to their poetics without pause to mull over the day, to succour a life wherever it may sponge the usage of an eye, not to make men ill but to use their blood as a carriage to their purpose. O it's the fool's paradise to emphasize his mutiny and accentuate his conceit to such a sterile eloquence that grangers would tremble to hear him speak of the heifer's haint. It's like the provost's pursuits of time and relativity, for in them that hear me rightly I am as a hellion in a spouse, stirring them with their previous conditions, holding them to the many mirrors of a fear. For truly what defends us keeps our fears as near to our ration as a shadow. Who would not fear a lion? But what dullard would fear it from a mountaintop? Tell me the Devil makes my ration keel, and I'll foxtrot to my own conceit. O they make me retch before a nun and call my providence a whore; they make me tally up my own uses as if I were a helot to use them on myself; they put strategies in my savagery and cunningness in my fears; they pull me to the doldrums and explain how I've been damned from birth by my own death for bucking back; they careen my dozy inhibition and make them dreams they do not dare desire on their heels. Think you my wisdom fears anything it understood before ever it was spoken? God, I forsake all my cram, which secedes you like the ghost who flickers my lights, I am your gentile swot. To light up the pergola of truth like a blind man in the Sun, is much to a madman's designation of what is and what is not. There lies complexity in simplicity's grave, in the satire of eloquence, which flusters appreciation with embossed elegies as touching as a murderer's last tribunal. It docks the concern of proof to yield a garden its damnation, merely because it importunes such a fantasy, it's a castle in the air. Like a self-conscious femme fatale hiding behind her pall, unkempt belief, in self-thwarted thraldom, trudges in the sunlight yet unfilial to its own disease of flies and maggots, for none shall know what schools the conscience of a dog. Is his fantasy not completed by the folio of one who will never know what thoughts his creed is made of truth? You are an open book, misunderstood by the pretext, baffled by the context. Only the blind believe in light, the daft believe in sight alone. I would issue a fatwa on your head but your mind is as empty as silence. It's as molten as a wet rag on the Devil's head, for I must cool myself before I lose my mind. I have heard too many proverbs at once to specify the earthwork, which I pan and slate like a Dickensian poltergeist. I'll bind you to your own conscience like a mortise lock on your brain. It must cloister your remorse that you are like a crustacean destroyed by his own scabbard. I impede your temperance, that I might skewer your broiled spoonerism, like a half-warmed fish or a half-farmed wish, bound by the likes of words—scrofulous words, indignant in their claims, which bivouac in the semblance of their sort; scudding toward a singular metaphor like an old chi in the woods, an abiku, seeking out the Buddha's cause for happiness in his own godlessness. O how you bulge with presumption, concise to the blarney that makes of your doom the seduction of a cockatrice, from which you won't skedaddle without transmogrification, for to be godless from without is to be godly from within—lest you remain what you are. Your Grundyism is vulgar and earthy; your glares vile and loathsome; your words troubling to nothing deeper than the surface of a fear; your quintessence dead to every virtue that yields in those who know the gypper's scandal is falser to himself than anyone else. It's a fracas of the will. Truth could silence an auditorium of hypocrites and wise men alike—you have such ideas in your skull as my ethics could silence in a mere discourse of reason. No matter the will, what bequeaths him is the earth, for the proportion of a man's life is no greater than a grave. I would haul over the coals on this faith of yours, Lucifer, but I doubt you'd find the words to light a fire worthy of my fear, reaching deep into the catacombs of your will. It's not so elusory to find fault in every street and ghost-infested house, which the slums elucidate with their argot, their patois, their lingua franca, but what elutriates the squalor of these people from their humanity is in the eye of the beholder. I've seen much idyllic bane, but these people bear my sympathies as peasants do. Such a reel would catch a fish but then the fish would eat him whole. O God! Destiny's a peeress waiting to be woken to the task! Do not tell me I am mad, for my madness will say: I am not mad; I am able; and my ability teaches my madness to walk the line like a trapeze artist. From time to time a concord gathers in my skull, embargoed with a substance purer than a churchyard tree, penitent for having ingrained itself with sleep when knackered by a dream as deep as to the root. Like a Saviour reading ghost stories to the godless and giving visions to a dreamless brood of lazars, these things became hereditary to my blood, more grotesque to my soul than a polliwog growing to the size of a loch. A thought, which cannot hold itself against its own intelligence, inquires the astrologer and claims his knowledge epitomizes the stars. Don't rely on despair to give motion to its own paralysis. What more can I question in a grain of wit than a matter which to me is as real as a legacy left behind the sandman's presages? Ay, there's a peril in every query; it bides to eavesdrop on the hearts of liars, to hold them to their cards and play them for their honesty. The Modernist's literature is a fishwife who would not give a flyspeck about the folly of a netherworld monger, if he is but a rathskeller's drunkard. While I, abstemious to the bone, must know that the median is unbalanced. How can you find a place, if you seek it in its foreigner? Death is the foreigner in which we seek out heaven. Peace be unto you—I am dead of thought. A thought in matter is the matter in thought, but I can explain neither the matter nor the thought. What sickness could interiorize this noxious war of blood versus blood, vulnerable to this man's prose and that man's wisdom? Ay, the slow evolution of this idiopathic quarrel we call to life rests beyond the pact of a cursory idiom. Its sorrow is obdurate within this executive storm, and is but the penance of my dogtrot, and so it yields me but a dollop from the do-gooder's poser, which cannot otherwise proclaim the image. What justice have I in my stealthy knack that drags me through these times like a witch into the bonfire of her convent? Ay, like the kulak's precincts, wherein a tale-bearing butterflies bring peaceful nature the claims of a storm curling the skies a universe away. It's Lucifer's magnum opus! Ay, such an barren age we have here at our beck that we can't smell the rot without becoming rotten ourselves. I'll cavil and caveat any man who argues with my quota, that I am no more a monger of reason than a cockatoo on the asymptote of the universe, who dreams its songs a hundred leagues above the century to make its music comestible to the divine. Don't squib my thoughts like an ancient daydreamer, sequacious to the tee. Ah, fiddle-de-dee, I fibrose my most flammable interjection and set fire to the terms, but I'll not dine at the devil's slab like an ordinary sinner, a desperado in the desert. I'll seriate myself to the sequela of my wit, through peccadilloes and the gift of tongues, though the words be heavenly, they've not fallen from the eyrie like eggshells to a snake . . . does that make me God's eyras or his circuitous teller of pixie tales? My love's enteric; it's a plea to keep myself as I wish to be; it's a word struggling to become an echo in my heart of hearts. I envy any man who has not been genuflect for a desire that kills all desire. But jealousy is a ranting termagant in perfect suspicion of her love; you would think she is become Jupiter's elixir, a Utopian bootlicker whose dialect is flung unto others as God's catharsis for the status quo. A Messiah among the gentiles, who somnambulates across my span to make me think you are awake and to steepen my fall. Am I compunctious to you now that I am honest; or does the honesty speak to make me a better man? There's no strata from here unto death; don't absquatulate from your grave to a life of riches; the earth judges no man according to his estate, it can only take what is flesh and bone. Death isn't worth a sesterce to Caesar, but to me it's a protectorate where the spirit freely roves, where it ranges invisibly like a swathe in the sand. The difference between a genius and a greenhorn is a mere process of the mind: do you think in squares or roots? So far we have been stars baffled by our own capacity for light. It is by wondering where this perception came from that our perception goes to waste; it is by wondering what we are that we cannot know? Wonder is not a bridge; it is a river dreaming up a bridge above itself to answer the shore on either side. So far, as a name, you would drag God through the depth of hell and gently sing the lauds of angels like a thief in heaven, with nothing but heresy as your heart's affidavit . . . Everything you have ever admired in any man, all the rage, you have seen in Jesus, and what is within him came from His Father. If you are to gentrify the stoke of luck you disperse on the gambler's table, should you not bridge these chances with your knowledge of the game? It is to climb to the unknown by what we know. O God! My mind is split into halves! The Draconians do their own will according to their own truisms, bunking off into oblivion like Hamlet's impasse. O God . . . I do Your will. The things to come must reveal themselves through subtlety, but I am not disposed. You're unapprised of the occasion that haunts you like a midnight poltergeist. Genius is an exploit from the precincts of others; you must keep a tight rein on your own mind. It is by what others have known that you sprout your kernel, though I fear the conscience of an illiterate spirit awaits me in my sleep. Even Argus cannot seem to see it. Do you find solace in the blind man's philology—it winces my farmhands of storytelling, which in this callused disgorging of words, is as the veneer of confusion upon the lowlier agreement. When you understand this, you'll see me no more as a tyro on the roof, but as a don to myself. Genius is nothing more than a divergence of the will, a simile of sorts; it is a mare and a snail in a steeplechase. It's a ghost in the woods, a posteriori, a priori, Abanddon in Elysium. To speak is an act of faith; to be heard is the soul's equivocation. It is God's quail to be of such an echelon as to not be understood by the meek. Ay, but why are you making inroads for the rest of us to follow? There, in the glum of mediation, lions would be so tame as to congregate with their quarry. Your ego suppurates before us like a pregnant nun, action supplies us with our doom's silver salver, from which we spurn our casual ordnance with the sputum of heavy decisions. But who can outthink a takeoff's wind-up, a Rabelaisian thinker such as Lucifer himself. The poet denies his hitch ascertains a deeper snag, termed loosely as the labour of deceit, still can drape sporadic thoughts with flowery wafts of greenery, as though the Arcanum could resolve his lightless dispute with light. Thus why settle yourself, wingless as a sponge, when you can fly freely in a Universe intended for wonder's departure into the mysterious sky? Politics is the acme of the revolution, like the theatrics in the skirmish of words between no-thinkers and yes men. It's the utmost quirk upon the quark, like tied-in histories waiting to be acknowledged by an honest historian. Who are we then, when our thoughts are not our own? Think like a thimble;

the world's hopes are to coax your perfection to stillness; to put a needle in your haystack and show you how your dumbness is bolder than a concubine at a pub of cowards, as consistent as a churl to the idols of his rancour, his soulless acrimony. Who does wisdom barter with, that his trolls, aloof as the nightly glum make occurrences of his deceit, troubles of his tales, to clone themselves till doomsday? Who does this creed misplace to such a loss of mores, that his honour, though it sits pensive in his persona like a china doll, descends to his pluck away his chutzpah? Your soul is trapped in the interim of faith and doubt; the mirror, your reflection will teach you how to die like an image, since you have lived as nothing else. How do say such a thing without setting a mirror to your insult? Talent scrounges; Genius creates its own craft like a witch's cauldron in winter time. It kicks up a fuss in our very brains. Think you I envy the intangible gallimaufry, the redundant talk of revolutions without ideas? I gallivant around gardens and smell what others smell, see what others see, and feel what others feel, but I cannot nor desire to think what others think. Thinking is art's repletion, beauty's debt to a mentalist's unwilling reality. Perplexity tweaks the lover's apoplexy to become the torrent of powerful pauses, like a crypt that rises within the memoirs of a dead man, who claims to hide his prophecies in the future of discovery. (...) I'm a hermetic Chapman, an anchorite, a nomad in God's somatic dream, a thief in search of something mysterious, which becomes a sort of self-mirage. Disabled by the fear of being disabled, I walked on the pathless path like an empty-minded lazar from here to there but finding nothing in between. *"Meaningless, meaningless, everything is meaningless," says the Teacher.* But his meaninglessness was never meant to be. My thoughts were like tyros trying to act out the parts of a complexity they couldn't understand—and so my paradox kept changing like a transient dimension. In states of hypomania, my Spirit was made purblind, by the incubus that embodies Dead Sea politicians, deriding the dust in each other's pathways—though dust is always the same no matter how you look at it. The two voices in my head were like Palaeozoic philosophers arguing about the texture of the light, the depth of the well, the existence of God. I became comfortably numb within myself, like a fly in a caste of amberoid, I couldn't even sense the coming of the spider. My mind became the only place for conversation, describing itself to the secret silence of its own enigma, like a self-conscious mirror in search of its true reflection, but finding it nowhere, seeing nothing except the nothingness within itself. Life became nothing more than a forgetful memory . . . and it suborned me to peek into my mind like an unknowable messenger, and find that the stairway, not its descent, was what I feared the most—merely the possibility of the descent, into the darkest depth, into the realm of absolute oblivion, no longer aware of Cyprian sweatshops, or Al Capone presidencies, each of them treading each other's heels like demi-god hell-hounds, to accomplish the *abomination that leads to desolation."Are you not mindful of your own mind?"* saith the spirit of a man, and from his carbon mist I heard de Molay's ghost decry: *What is it that this world forgot that the Son of Man himself can't find refuge in the churches built upon His Word?* Ay, life to me was a faux-naif mime who performed my likes and dislikes whether I liked it or not. But however severe the malaises of the collective mind, I traveled on, wearied by the imagoes of God, yet entranced by the ideal of some noetic Otherworld, not quite nolens volens, but somewhere in between each notion, willing to speak but unwilling to be heard. Life incurred a literature I condemned within myself to understand the very depths of Hell, meanwhile Heaven hovered somewhere above my knowledge, like God's noli me tangere awaiting His re-birth in nature's ovum. Dyslexic to God, I dug a labyrinth within myself to elude His eye, even though there was nothing to fear—the incubus only existed insofar as I was willing to hide. But a man lost in the melodrama of his own fantasies, fears himself like a self-conscious ghost in a samizdat fire, replicating the dreams of a no-hoper before the many mirrors of a fear. The Man on the podium is as insightful as his outlook, and he repeats himself as carefully as a geometric satrap near a map, basking in the capriccio of publicans and Pharisees, handing out invisible pamphlets printed by Morgan le Fay's scepter to the unsuspecting proletarians of mass and distribution, to spread an eclipse that would blind the hungry and hunger the blind. But God's Eye kept watch over the dwindling golden road and before the haunted forest He openly declared: BEWARE THE ONE-EYED MERCHANT!!! His consciousness is more invective to native silences than the throes and nightmares of a prelapsarian shaman, who secludes the talking ghosts of the past to a velvet room where music cannot possibly be sound. Does the mood create the world or the world create the mood? *"If you tap upon an empty jar,"* says he, *the emptiness mourns the echo of existence."* He differs with a difference, and teaches blindness never to settle for its groping. The Hoodoo Man's mirage expends our convictions by force-feeding us false hope—Pontius Politics! Ay, the mind becomes a self-enraptured circus, a highbrow chimp being brainwashed at a Chaplin flick! *Moloch! Moloch! The Keeper's in the Clock! And the Wicked Witch of the Western World knows the Pontiff like the husband she defrocks!* God's light to me questioned my pain like an unsatisfied mystery, despising my conscience like some Blind Freddie, in a selfsame prison where over-informed citizens talk about politics for the rest of their knowable lives. Each day my happiness suffered like a burning vesture, and each day I added to the fires of its riots, white as a blind man's blitzkrieg, like some absurd Gotterdammerung domed by germanium witches, whose spell assumed it would never be broken, nor unspoken, awaiting some pre-estrus political god who proofreads his propaganda to the living relics of his lost disciples: *"The instruments of peace are necessary to preserve the war. The instruments of peace are necessary to preserve the war."* Like one who, weary of the night yet dreams himself within it and sets his moorings so deeply into the grounds of his deceit that no truth ever escapes him, the Man is a prisoner in a rogue's gallery, a shirker of shame, unwilling to damn his soul but acting upon the dearth like a sick little peasant child, a mischievous recreant entranced with the Spirit of Fear, with the speech of agnostic angels, inciting the clouds to rain upon the neediest seeds of his dementia, like an arrant armyworm's navigation through unsettled fields of dust. His sapience, like a dying old man at a bugaboo rally, fills his pate with the knowledge of a dead man, yet, like a trapeze artist on a tightrope set afire, he concedes his victuals to be wary of any loss that wages itself against the *memoirs* of his *struggle*, to be as exact in guilt as a portion of lust weighed against the desires of a lecher. And so the Oligarch's magic spell led astray the dying, like Machiavellian monks in black-light monasteries, with a yellowed Timbuktu map and a grey zone compass, that the living might never know what is to become of them until they die. But, verily, I say: *"In the tribunals of Left versus Right, the only way out is Up!"* For a man and his disaster, himself oblivious of his mien, goes to his grave unfathomed of the deed that damns him. It's the everlasting idleness of a man in the everlasting desert of himself, to become a heptahedral augur made spendthrift by doubt, by fear, by a Revelation that the Anointed Ones must never dare to speak: We will no longer die for Caligula, nor wield to the endless charades and bargains of the One-eyed Merchant, nor wend down godless paths that chase felicities to their graves, nor give our grief to devils and inquire them like old institutions of truth, nor reckon with every fire that threatens the Houses of Balaam, nor misconstrue the diaphanous faces of Zion as the elders of Barabbas, nor misguide the grace of prophets through the idioms of

Baal, nor inveigle Peace like an old mistress that we'd never dare to love or understand, nor incite ourselves to outrage beyond the circumstances of our own mores, nor converse of pointless errands that vainly try to originate from the Unknown, and return with no knowledge of the life that never ceases to inquire the Abyss where no life enters. *"Let the dead bury their own dead!"* (…) A long time ago I was a poet with no Odyssey. I sang Anchises' songs, feeding silage to my enemies. I'm a man without a soul, no feelings to control, And I've found my fardels of acumen, like a fish caught by a tole. Hate consumes what's left of you, like a snake inside a petrel's egg. You're a mystery with a mind, baffled by the things you find. There's a conflict if interest, and a fool's paradise in each of us, Hegel's "Phenomenology of Spirit" is on the rise here, there, and everywhere . . . like Huxley's excursion through the Doors of Perception. This is the end of post-modern relativism. I hold the keys of Death and Hades, and I've come to destroy those who destroy the Earth . . . Dylan's here to fill the void with poetic justice, like a dead mime in a practitioner's cage. He stole all my swansongs with his time machine, and now I'm dying like an old man in a church. He's the quintessential New York hipster . . . and he was given a boost of Shakti, like a shaman in a wool-gathering reverie. We see intimations of a new world view, and the passion of the western mind . . . it's our time now . . . the Age of Aquarius is upon us. My brain is on the fritz in the Gaslight Café . . . I've got a revolution in my head and a buzzing in my ears. Uranus and

Pluto are aligned as a square, it's the Dust Bowl all over again . . . so let us be inspired by the sixties like Renaissance artists as we await the Bohemians year after year. Meanwhile reality is unconvincing unless your dreams come true . . . Helter-skelter has become your state of mind, here, now and forevermore. I want to listen to music sometime in the future that I might know what I should listen to ahead of time. Long ago I fell in love with Sad Eyed Lady of the Lowlands. A shiksa goddess with an upside down brain and a mercury mouth . . . I want to die like a poet in the ghetto . . . where I saw an Art Deco Nazi train full of Jews. In the desert I ate locusts and wild honey, waiting for the return of Christ . . . when I died my soul travelled through an Einstein-Rosen Bride all the way to Pleiades . . . the mystery of the seven stars was in my hands. Doing the undoable and thinking the unthinkable . . . until death do us part, like Blake's Marriage of Heaven and Hell. I will destroy the wisdom of the wise; the intelligence of the intelligent I will frustrate . . . to raise the dead you must first disbelieve the Death—this dictum is dead to he who remains in disbelief. What is timeless is timeless because truth cannot disregard its own idyllic nature. We must live but mustn't desire the life within us, lest we lose our will to live whenever the desire forsakes us. To make-up your own world is to be at odds with the status quo, to thereby change society by showing it its own reflection. Man lives in such a way that he would sooner die than reveal his secrets to the world—like the Devil's advocate, they seek to destroy the man they represent. I beg my loneliness to leave me alone, like a spirit that assumes the presence of an unknown man. Vanity is so often glorious that glory itself becomes the vanity. could return with an acoustic guitar. But what's a bred-in-the-bone poet to the world nowadays but a tired old Brechtian soul, who feeds his moments ekdam like Schrödinger's cat, alive and dead at the same time in different dimensions, and poses questions to the most unnecessary of his troubles for the sake of eloquence? We ignore our way to self-destruction on peyote by walking backwards toward the edge of a crag. A gambler is a pilgrim who loses everything in his way and loses his way to recover what he's lost. After a while reality becomes an unconvincing proxy to its own suppositions. Anger makes us hew the pursuit from the follower—as if the follower is to blame for the pursuit. Anxiety is more apt to agree with the tradesmen than to question his trade; even as his trade brings you to ruin within yourself. Absinthe confuses the liar who lives inside your Impressionist brain, who bides by laws that no longer make any sense. like a mysterious man heading toward the unknown, life wends down the stairways we dare to question, but never quite to the depth of the answer. A poet should always have something to keep mum, something that the recipient cannot quite receive unless he himself is open to the insight. The mind only becomes apparent to itself when time and space no longer matter. It's matter over mind. A storyteller is like a sullen recitalist; everything he does is in defiance of your expectations, like a fantasy performing in front of an invisible audience, whose own fantasies reveal it to itself like a chi in front of a broken mirror. A song is like birdcage seeking redemption not in the birds it could've caught but in erasing the bars between life and art. The mind is a haunted hostelry; madness walks in circles in its own sanatorium. It wilfully ignores the possibility of other rooms, where, if fate be bold, you will find yourself not as you imagined but as you truly are. It baffles a brute to suggest he's brutal; it baffles a liar to suggest he's lying to himself. Life is a tenor, at once the voice of one and many, tending to the crowds with an unseen vendetta—as gravity proclaims its law upon the mass of a feather, it is as helpless to the fall as a man to the crying soul of a broken-hearted songstress, who seeks what she cannot foretell more deeply than what she can—artlessness is the way of life's true artists. Truth assimilates man's conjecture. No man can undo another man's belief, but surely he can convince him to die for its sake. The tyrant says that there is no Truth beyond him, he is at once the messenger and the message, the undeniable hand that clutches gypsies' curses and sends them back to the lazars in the streets of Sodom and Gomorrah, saying to the helpless that they are free, and tergiversating to the hopeless that they are wiser than the helpless. Life disappoints you every time it meets your expectations. The past is the ghost that keeps forgetting to disappear, until the present reminds him he isn't here. A man may kill the wrong demon, fetch the bird that caused him no trouble, and yet be satisfied at the triumph of his vanity. Wisdom is to realize you've known nothing that isn't moot. We are tribes of doubt awaiting rainfall to confirm that the oceans disappeared according to our traditional expectations of water. Like tribes in use of useless passions wisdom dispels the stratus of our minds and rains upon us like an ancient mystery. Leisure is a gumshoe in an unmysterious room full of books he's already read. God absolves what is timeless and puts everything else aside. The observer always wants to become the observation, to no longer question the distance between his mind and reality. Enlightenment is to experience the universe while feeling no need to understand it. Self-sympathy is lewder than death in a dreamless crowd. Birds and fowls would not want to live in a world where music is nothing more than a sales pitch to the snakes. A fool doubts everything he doesn't see that he might deceive himself to know all things as they are. No one ever strays from what they think is true. As soon as the path becomes familiar, all learning ceases and we forgo our purpose for a false sense of ownership. Life is the mystery that knows exactly what you must become in God's eyes. Politicians put progress on a treadmill, and say the economy is on a strict regiment. We've been dying in self-imagined wars, like vagabonds tempting death into each other's houses for what is of no worth to any other moment in history, and trying great fates merely to dissuade the quotidian in which we all pretend to do good work. Every great mind is known merely for its interim in great matters. We are a great complexity trying to live simple lives, like self-intrigued mysteries learning that nothing else is out there. To the Spirit, gold ingots are as worthless as dirt. Man must learn to recognize pain as the dryad that leaves him with more wisdom than it came with. Madness is a cyclical ghost who returns only when it must confront its own reflection. Don't be frugal when the truth is spendthrift, lest your frugality deprives you of reason. Only when the artist truly disappears does his art become nascent. Acting is to act as though you are not acting. Our will suffers us like a lonely old man at a bazaar who ponders his purpose beneath a sickly cloud called Fate; who could be led to his mind down such a mindless conduit? Fear is more gullible than a fish in a dried up pond. The drab pretence of wishful mysteries, cannot change man's unique ambition to be better than himself, hoping for things beyond man's knowledge that haunt his imagination like a sceptre in a well. There is no unknown beyond men's minds, only within does our knowledge await us. You are the mystery that regrets the intrigue, the clue that doubts the assertion—a man standing in a weakening ray of light who yet believes he will never die. A hypocrite is a self-righteous mirror unto every man but himself, not for similitude, but merely to avoid living by his own philosophy. What suffering his intelligence must endure that it has to imagine itself altogether. Your mind, for now, is a lazar who is at once lame and blind but someday, through faith in itself, it will walk and see like Lazarus. Only the blind believe in light; but that doesn't mean light doesn't exist. Originality should never be able to recognize itself. Consciousness works where working is the worker's existence. Life needs no escape, unless you've imagined the cage. You can't be happy and evil at the same time. I believe in everything; therefore everything exists. Hieronymus says greatness comes only by the recognition of others, when they see their own potential in another man's dreams. Understanding proves identical in God and man, the math problem solves itself the same in either mind. Life is a great striving toward nothingness. Madness is the mismanagement of your own mind. The past is a prison in which the future contemplates its life. Through a garb of intellect or colloquial dust given to the winds of speech, no tree would confound its own fruit to famish the roots of knowledge. There is no such thing as a mystery, only inexperience. Like a cherub's diurnal fantasies of flight, or the gastropod's classic trail, where it lollygags in ancient malathion. It mews the protean theme in the thespian father's art, as though a simple flame could gut away the sea. No man has seen infinity who has not looked into the eyes of God, like that sad septentrion star, where the galls of hebetude could never dote their absolution on lacunas that refuse the cosmic bridges of space-time. Lucifer's perception divulges what God refuses to reveal to man . . . who yet can read the genizah like a mystery set afire, but what trammels the dirges of this travesty, if not by plundering her tutorial spheres whose imagination could teach a star to imitate her poise? But never could they bereave the twilight of her eyes to fetch the unrequited wonder of my own. I will not cozen your otiose tryst, or discipline the outcome, or when circumstance judges the conduct it once conceived, minds shiver to witness irony's parody on

Sense. I obverse justice to my impatience to know that I, my own heart's outcast, exiled in yours, must find proclivity in self-wallops of penance, is as degrading as the dying posture of a rose, yet illative of such a death as lovers may choose. In dreams, sylvan birds can't exclaim Autumn's tirade against Summer's togs of greenery, though the tocsin's weep inside the ivory tower. Nature's demerit suffers the sensorial trims of time, when Winter's vesicant breath jabbers our Venusians tragedies. What knowledge owns men so deeply that they fib the clue and refuse to swim above Truth's surface, where things are real, not thought of to exist, like the panzer's strategies, or the recluse's pawky masquerade, or the pen pusher's prosody. Let them sab the prowl of a look, and in it read the gnomic passado of their disparagement. Such hysterics make fallacy pursy with self-destruction, as a leaf would apportion its death to its own resistance against Fall. Past thoughts are leaves that no longer require their mind, whose inaction pursues forbearance to forbear its pursuance. If ever I suffer the instinct of conscience, more like a thief than a boggler to reason with, I will fall away into madness. O madness, the mind's peregrination through Lucifer's perception, to seem as deified as Nero's quondam copycats, whose wanderlust would study the wainscots within his all-fired proem. This consummation assails sorrow's eclogue and trestles their wonder. The hoodwinker's politics and his balks of bathephilous tears prods their intelligence, as though uncultured procedure could howk out our spoon-fed sprigs of conscience. I inquire no more, lest I kill what I sought to understand, and understand what I sought to rebuke. And so I peer into the abyss of pulchritudinous mysteries, wherein we question the rose to doubt its smell exists. O Death, do you sashay with such prodigal cause, with the Dacron's prose left to question our denial, to make of Perception our tarpaulin's shadow, if we are to ascertain the mystery of our lives irony would drown a fish in its own bowl. Silence is a penance to the soul, and it's in the phatry of that craw that Truth must dwell. O self-suspicious conscience, like the sedimentation of stones craftier than their crafter, let us not behoove ourselves: from dust we came and to dust we shall return. Eternity awaits us in self-apothegm whereon the wistful badinage of sleep beaches its most liberal leviathans. Nostalgic maguey at last may wink its sovereign eye, with an electoral pugilism. There's an elixir in Art: when the artist disappears, the art's purer to the kin, more deeply taken than the senses. But must I, like an noxious gizzard, digest every color that the chameleon takes from nature, to know how it bevels the credence, like a ghost who lunges at everything death will take away from him? Art's in dire need of self-reckoning; we must set aback the antics of mediocrity, which mimics the eccentricities of the greater mien like a self-conscious mime with gestures disproportionate to the presentment. His altruism's in cahoots with the wrong words and yet you give them meaning! O God, I cannot quote what currently flubs my brains! It's madness; I am mad! O God, God . . . it holds such a distort in my gall that there's no other Dame or

Mistress in all the starry assemblage of my spirit that could hold me such a pawn in my own desires. O God . . . I am like Daedalus in an invisibility mantle! Pathos to you then, this timely peerage is no longer your scruple. I suffer like a lightning bolt holding lectures on the surface of a lake, yet you debase it to a millivolt on a mere. The time has come to change a lascar into a god, not by his capacity but by the religiousness of his tripe. You would pontificate a libel and make it holy by the burning whispers of a witch in a basilica. The yob's destiny, the fate of the oaf, cannot see the altar as a catalyst of sufferance until it convokes in his vanity, since to worship such a vanity is to make it holy by the Passion of the Christ. Am I a ghost in a husk of life? This diatribe's a fable to you, since you refused to believe its provenance was love as raw as an unseasoned venison in a lion's mouth. You've strained the diapason of an angel and held choirs to her ears for the sake of God. If that my love could sing like a cognoscente, I would be like a ghost in heaven. You would think the bodice makes the woman and please her with a dress, all the while neglecting the apparels of her duplicity, a convocation of lust and petty rituals set beneath the baldachin you made with the starlight fires. You'd breathe in the balbriggan of a whore and sing to her allure until the satisfaction silences your oriole-like dishonesty, and shame congregates in your after-dinner congress of lies . . . now, since your bandolier's been emptied, perhaps she thinks how the excuse of a bore would have bettered your performance. It's your madness that speaks. I wouldn't thrall madness to his labour were he not forgiven in my mind's most haunted corridors—who then will barge upon the trials of heaven, when freemasons disclaim its deception and sire us beneath ascension's borne? They cannot cleave to their oblivion without changing the plenum's disagreements on reality, so who can cease the reaper's daily slog, when the leisure would cease him whole? If death to nous abjures no question to the grave, what would flesh chastise in the wind, when it carries our cares to another place? This isn't the seeming of the panorama. May I have a grog to quench my thirst? How grody must you be to become your own bone fide? The trouble is laden with its own distrust of reality; the disposition is heaped like its pogrom's bones. Here comes the corollary, like a hawk in search of inquisition; or a crook in search of a better life to purloin; a spirit in search of a voice as tender as the ear, whose echoes will not return to deny its existence; a prophet in search of a road that he cannot predict to the doomsday of itself, lest he forebodes himself to no one. It's easy to suppose oneself as anything; all you need is a little bit of convincing. I'm a zhlub: I must zazen myself to refresh my wits. O damn me to this fantasy like a drab in a secret convent, damn me to this life like a mistress in the asters, to your untenable junctures of time and fervour unexpended! Put a mirror to it! For a man must go backward to know he's heir to his own decisions. This posit justifies itself like mercy in a dungeon . . . thoughts, to be acidulous at best, censure our fears more aptly than the banker's bluff, as though the pools of Sodom redact our tears from the plummet of their depth. Fear is more gullible than a fish in a millpond; truth uses my own lies against me. A closed door must hold the secrets of the room. A choice in matter matters most. You must suffer the same disposition that even Hamlet could not overthrow. Did he ever lack a word? But do not call me his avant-garde quondam, for I was not born to be like him, but to be so much unlike him that his ghost would seek my mystery to know why Atlantis drowned him in the dust of angels, and baptized me to be an alguacil of semblance. What's your hokum? Hoke it out like a man in a maelstrom. He knew all the methods of prose and quip . . . but he knew no more about happiness than a dead man's wish knows where it is received, transmogrified in's grave by his corpse's effluvium—is it you who adulates God's smarting? Is it you who reasons with our mordancy, as though our senses were the strontium of your mindless white wash. Hamlet knew no other way to grow but to drown himself in so much knowledge that madness overflowed his cognizance like the blood of an imagined pogroms. What man could abide this constancy, witnessing the same foolishness day after day, and not forsake this reality for the troubles of his own mind like an overheated hors d'oeuvre? I'll no longer hide my certainties in a porter's pail, destined for the well of ineptitude. If a blind man discovered heaven, he could never describe it to any other man. So mallow your heart with the urchin's imagination if you must. But no larrikin should decry the road with his fetid stench, prettified by eloquence that deifies its happiest tryst to the

Unknown. Maladroit and, with his strategies as imperative as war, he straddles along great catastrophes like a belief on a tight-rope traipsing toward the other end. Make of fear your mind's acerbic vicar; a parson who says anything that reveals him to the world, like a rector who, discovered, becomes something with power to his use, with sudden fervour whose gainsay would ridicule even he who speaks it. Like strange messengers in a stranger's fib, it's our daily requiescat . . . to believe that we are good, and that we bring favour to that quality by remarks that rile the others by hiving them off. But why frame the words that thief our hearts, when indehiscent seasons return to blossom in our skulls like the Garden of Eden? The songster's words, wrapped in a ceremony more clever than its dances, cannot be festive in a mind that has not felt the sway of his music. It's a mystery which needs neither solving, nor intrigue. If changes err against the exponents of the law, then I am not he who grates a postern to be of service to its secrecy. It is to mistake God's voice as your own, like an ancient bloomer in the heart, and repeat it to the world as an original gen. Let it plummet in the meaning, branded for definitions now the wont of antediluvian rotes—why would a gist enthrone two-facedness? O frailer than this is the lover's gorgon, which is nothing but two disagreeing horsemen on the same horse! Humdrum! Leave me to my own desolation; like a itinerant, I'll solve it with my own mind somewhere along the way. Ideas, though lugubrious in forte, are like a lagoon, the surface is always troubled, but never the depth—it is always at peace like a cleric in the ecclesiastic moonlight. O that you could see what unseeing portends—by fain, it buoys them to stride the hegira's itinerary. A wise man, adjusted to the incongruous task of a Saviour, like a dollop given to a gravedigger after a holocaust, will refuse any death that does not give him God. What worse thought eases itself into the mind's ellipsis: the one that in thinking uncovers a path as iniquitous as the old one, or the one that creates a new way to approach questions of life? This disease possesses him like a spirit, who wakes where his mind falsifies him to the world and tells him to disrobe the future to reveal the present day. It's too intrepid, too plucky to tempt exigency in cowards! What I must do to most men would seem a trifle of oddity, a foible, the very complexion of madness sneering at a choir of nuns. Aye, it's like a peddler who cannot cease his troubles unless he stops a-peddling. O that I were in a town of Bohemians instead of landed gentries. Aging wilts the brain to a sort of dementia that I cannot fathom in my youth. And so it is that art, as the gamut and continuum of our endless journey as souls lost in this the town of Amlethus. The spirit of a man enlightens him throughout his life. O Apollo, I think of you like a tyrant I have not power enough to depose. In our circadian hours, the cinch of the cerulean sky is still to eventuate our meteorological inklings. God's an ironist, a quirk of fate to say the least, and he's brilliant at hiding it, like the stars during the day. And so it is that the Draconians, Lucifer's entourage, these larva, breed beneath the earth, unknown as death to a dying man. This sulk, which, with eagerest threat, raring to go, forecast the seasons of my blood to a vengeance from a simple gall, a din from a tender melody, a twinge from a pleasure, an allure from an intrigue, take everything from nothing and do with it nothing more, leaving me blameless yet guilty all at once. O vanity sleeps in my mores like a broken eggshell, to flex the oppressor's dreams; it enwraps my fears to give them bodies with which to skip and boogie, it speaks in my involuntary mind and trembles in my nightmares as though it had not borne them, like a magician who claims no wonder to his tricks while the glory's his to reckon on the crowd. It'll ponder me like a madness, swallow me like the leviathan's gullet, chase me like the conscience of an Amlethian Gonzo. There's an omniscient spell in the exploit of a man, that his mind no longer wakes in his own life, but in his trek's verve, lost like a sprog's ghost. O let inspiration gibe nature's requiem; let it promise bewilderment to explorers of the dust by which no coaxial notion grows among the dead. There is a dream, faraway and varied by motley indicters, whose sleep pans us from our own—it veers our most honest discourse toward our last recourse! If melees come, let them also dispirit their own ways; I am not pat to those who would slash and hack my gardens. But who dares dream up a brigand in himself, knowing he'll pilfer their ideas. My mind is whetted by the knack. O is this not the place where death takes me for my wonderment? I'll have my vengeance! O how strangely a bugaboo's exertion lunges at my conceit like a widow! For I am the ghost who keeps forgetting to disappear, until something reminds him he isn't here. Thy Will be done, not mine. O God, God, wherefore art thou God? Secret solaces afflict any heap of dust we may become, and your name is often but a word, whose meaning we cannot host without a foreign pang into the very heart of the matter. O God, God, wherefore art thou God? Is it the temperance, or the caws of a Sibylline crow that embargo our orisons like muddled curses, like one making woe unto woe, and silence unto silence? It is familiar, though distance suggests no deference of reaction, that every sunset births no septentrion star, but a mullion brewing the changeling's airs like a cosmos concoction; it is what ravishes in our tears, that sufferance clings and sorrows hunch beneath our embrasures, like inactive prose envisioning dreams of unspeakable death, embracing any limit we transgress, without dual choice, now become the burden of our lives. He who swaggers like a swag in the rain, joggles underneath his flesh, and suffers the cloak of mystery. We wear it like a homogeneous garb, and labour beneath the Sun's odium, despoil whatever happiness we aver with Sodom and Gomorrah's simplest pleasures. Peaceful in myself, at quarrel with the world, like an underwater fowl who yet does not desire the flight, I am left to ask the question: O God, God, wherefore am I Man? What is greatness in a man that it swags his goodness altogether, by whose words duplicity lends its hand to a self-baffled Book, till I die and the world knows me for my spirit? O let me widen my wonder like a polished ore, for answers are as portly as their questions—they blow breezes into our brainstorms, ethics in our volition. O soul, I am a lighthouse in search of God. Ay, we suffer an unintelligible existence; our sufferance reads us like blether on a parallax. But we will not feel the impact; no, not until we know what it strikes has resonance at all. Ergo, I am no one . . . as books are their authors, I am the life within me. Death too will give me many books, but these too will haunt haunts beyond the assortments of my guilt, in minds beyond my age and causerie. For death takes me as its prologue, and I do trudge this daily plight with too much passion, too much anger to remain still in my own mind. Be I the better half of myself, I know nothing other than the darker part. It is the criterion that beggars take to bed with them, that I am left to boondoggle my wit through these times like one dragging his own soul through the mud and dirt merely to absolve some sort of expiation. Am I so astounded to the grit, so perfectly dazzled by unknowable events that I must share myself with a messenger that I do not myself disavow? O you must be in the most piteous of moods to frazzle my certainty with these interludes. You're a scallion of sly and interminable looks, bridging dynasties together where no traveler reposes to reconsider his goings like an empty wharf. Do me the justice of leaving my life to my own hands and I'll have no straw against you to make your treasons do their dealings. Summon in me no more than you can snip with, for I am not bothered by your censure. What lives within me lives within me however it pleases; I have no accord, that fellowship belongs to God. I give him my body, my soul, but He cannot spare my sanity one moment at a time? This town's got a grasp on my memory like the devil's mare on a kindred spirit—though I share none of his abundance.

(...)

If the Sun cannot practice the ethics of light, what edacious abyss of selflessness shall not sclerotize its black heart, that its raconteurs might further macadamize the mysteries that are beyond death's borne? O honest lovers . . . never the twain shall meet! It shrives the merit of a blag without flinching, whose gumption soars through my deepest interim like a falcon in the hour of its death. To me there's a reverie in the sky when a falcon falls, a trance, a woolgathering of the senses . . . I judder with the same truculence when I lose a thought somewhere I may never rootle again. Who else could I meet to rival such a flair as yours? They would dwindle and lessen the degree of my interest to a nullity. Yours keeps rising . . . without explanation, without the relief of your fiendish presence. I keep predicting what you jot down like a literary medium, as though the foreground held your footsteps where you've never walked like a phantom in the dead of night. Love hushes a man's most desperate harangues, which is at the end of his tether. It codifies a prophecy to desire what it cannot foretell more deeply than what it can. But all such thinking must cease, for when first the path meets the brain's proviso. Love? You'd call my muse a blatant skinflint, a curmudgeon whore! Don't knap my skull merely to flummox the residue of a tear, if the feint embitters my response; for the mind and the brain exchange ideas like the sky and sea trade raindrops. It's what wearies us, for how can we find gurgled meanings in divinity, if manmade moments define eternity like a gurdwara in seventh heaven? Have we not all worn Beelzebub's wimple, when we heard the cries of our crooning hearts, sweeter than mildew or liquor to a gnat? Tell me, for surely it bodes that sweet primeval fire, which still burns within the stars, where words, unruffled by the claims of hellfire, pass their political pause within love's licentious brogue. O words, seek you quarrel in my silence or silence in my quarrel? I am a bitter, bitter ghost of equipollence and electricity! Literature sleeps in the interstice of love and makes us hew the pursuit from the pursuer, the follower from the followed. I wish I could dream up the room in which quantum poets speak new languages to themselves, in which originality can never recognize itself, like a mysterious man heading toward the unknown. I wish I could tell God about all my pointless journeys to the stairways I've feared and questioned, but never quite to the depth of the answer. It's too hammed, it's gravid of too much tenet that beggars would uphold in bellyaches. Gussy up a prosody like Rimbaud's Illumination, if thoughts unknown to you are dead, then what are you to them that they belly you like a foreigner in your own land? A gumshoe to silence? Politics is as a harlot's troubled conscience, which narrates its emaciation when victuals seem a mortal sin to the apple of my eye. Life's bestial outlook on the human quo warranto proposes men's deaths to be done in causal order, like a quodlibet in a songster's muse. But what balks us more deeply than hell's battalions can war with our souls, prods our intelligence, as though uncultured procedure could howk out our spoon-fed sprigs of conscience, and replant the Tree of Knowledge in the Garden of Eden. What shall we do if God fructifies our palms with our first temptation? We are made efferent by the worm's edentulous mouth, for war has kept its dead for all of history. It's a Weltschmerz as deep as the bottom of my heart. Nature welters the respect that this particular story suffers like the cloak of a ruffian tragedy, whose skulduggery weaves the plot from beginning to end like an angry idol in the desert. My consciousness is like a setting surrounded by biblical ghosts of Zion, those sceptres of dust, cannot haunt the corpses of words with more pun than the practice may claim in its wake, and yet they defrock death's translators like a society of dead poets. Everything is made of light. Whether adversaries bless each other's truths or transgress dreams beyond their surmise, the mystery's like an Illyrian tongue, passé in the modern epoch. It seems the spelunker's confusion is true, since he can find the grotto he has been seeking. We wend down roads we understand as much as the fools before us. O the sinner's exclaustration is a dalliance to usual mélange of literature, when Homer's return is like a cock-a-hoop transgression lined along the trenches of his lexicon, to grow into a mystery rose near a dalles. With such codswallop failing our Glagolitic faculties, intrigue is always beyond us. Truth suborns me to see my heart like a prayer that shells aberrations in a sinner, who speaks, heavier in tone than sincerity, deeper in look than thought, truer in form than sorrow. He dies by much the same myth as a cockatrice! Irony's the emperor of this world, yet the beggar of our littlest hub; it's so difficult to see but nothing sees life so clearly—for truth may be new to some, but to me it's as old as time itself. Mysteries are everything we desire within ourselves, like Christ betraying freemasonry's secret Word, or like the Ides of March to Brutus and his mob of conspirators. The paragon keeps repeating the quietus to the querist. Like a ley, at times my brain budges too much over the edge, it overspeaks, and underthinks, by whose intrigue a ghost town would disappear as soon as someone sees it; for as soon as there's a witness to the impossible, our minds go on to recount our former doubts as knowledge. Remorse no more could feel the thorn that would deracinate my conscience from the lustful rose of Sodom.

It's such a hokum in my brain that I can scarcely speak to it. God is somewhere in the futurity's panorama, waiting to be seen as He wants. During your session, you may as well have ripped out the entire Book of Revelations. If direction simplifies the road, I'll take you through the copse, the covert, the coppice; if you lose yourself, blame it on the ration. I'll be the one, on the bridges of dreams and cognizance, who holds a mosquito in a mildew saffron, to invent such a fiction in the eye that the mind would never dare to doubt. But whose knowledge preserves him to the world. Would acrobatic word-play tumble down the ages, like a phrase that adjourns itself to later symphony? O the sidereal simile cripples the able-bodied comparison, like stars too simple to fathom; who will ham the purposes of science, when fear is only supposed, only imagined in tomorrow's nature? The best way to learn is to lose oneself in the woods; paths are deceiving too many people into the pursuit of shadows. A musician, termed to his own minuets, mints his worth by the morrow's burr, his most sensitive plonk—like a phrase that adjourns itself to a another man's symphony. But the stars will never rehearse my wiles within the light; for as soon as the path becomes familiar, all learning ceases and we forget our purpose, like phantoms searching for life where nothing is hidden. Life is the mystery that knows exactly what you must become. Wherever you go, the life within you will always be the same, for the truth never changes; it only begins to purify you as soon as you realize it. It's the thunder without the lightning, an honour in no need of recognition, a window in love with itself, a ghost in a house long abandoned by the sun. I am proud; and I'm also dying at my nurse's hands. Is conceit of such amplitude within men that our kingdoms and the founders of our grace have grown their ethics on our oblivion? Ah, such is the vastness of man's mind. We've been treading on imagined surfaces, like a traveller oblivious to the depression of the town, and trying great fates merely to dissuade the quotidian, in which we all pretend to do good grafting. There is no such thing as progress until there is such a thing as expediency; and we, like answers parallel to our questions, walk each other by. Every great mind is known merely for its interstice in madness; but what gambler stakes his odds on powerless inklings and supposes the statutes of man morph themselves to his own purpose? Men are a great complexity trying to understand the simplest of their moments, still trying to understand the strangest ironies of life, like self-intrigued mysteries learning that nothing else is out there. What a pleasant bolt from the blue to have you back in the spectrum of your senses gawking down idly at the subconscious, which seemed to have possessed you so potently just a while ago. We rant our demons to all, like one who deceives the world to believe her mind is as a child's; magical though it proves nothing to a magician. When my mind is in perfect silence, I fear the memory of sound, like a backward fjord. I can't be happy in the parallax of dreams when the moments are simpler than I am. Like a trudge of fey in-taking the echoes, it goes to follow like a hollow man: ambition, then despair, then madness. It's the order of the mind. But I am not yet mad, I am an ego with a triage of thought to recognize pain as the imp leaves me with more wisdom than it came with. I'm frugal when the truth is spendthrift. I thought such a day would blind me, since it would be as a skit of nobilities that counter the gill; but it's true, we have at last encountered a woman who plays her role like one whose treble-mind is the design of hyperphysical jests and gainsays, a Chaplinesque heirloom to the silent theatre of knowledge. Mad thoughts to madmen seem as sane as sunlight. If it be so, I am mad as a harebrained madcap in a bedlam. Ay, apotage especial for your health, to put an end to the Draconian pong over Amlethian life. Indeed, time must endure the laws that import themselves into the soul of a man, like a serf in a hoosegow, pondering his own mind like a prehistoric wasteland. You are what you think, not what you think you are. Perception works where working is the worker's existence. Let the theatre cosset in the drama awhile: thinking's the trap, in which food for thought seems verbatim, but is only a matter of hunger. Ay, thinking, here too's the rub, young Hamlet. The Universe does not need us to exist, but without us it surely would be a void. But how so to argons of nature, who change for merriment that makes our fears surface in other ages, like bumblebees drowned in honeyed proverbs. The mind is capable of greater greatness, deeper depths, higher highs. God is the answer to all of life's questions. Like a maharishi's petroglyph, a metaphor is only what confirms reality as an idea, a predestined diagram of possibilities. Madness is one's observation and obsession for something which is untrue in the mind of God. You're dyed-in-the-wool pathology, like a linsey-woolsey of ration dipped in blood, won't streak your madness with so ghostly a charge, unless you've given your fears to your past and made your future suffer to speak the rite. Your dwaal, forming an eschar on your mind, has taken the shape of the memory, to think itself a more recent and more powerful presence, like an evil spirit eructed from your sense of self to let you admire that he possessed you as a man and left you as a soul. Your errantry's been doodled on the guest, to make him admire his own mind by exploring yours, like Shakespeare's daemon. How fortunate a gizzard you give me, that I've aged along with his wisdom instead of time. Riposte! Ay, there's a halon on the devil's heart. And so it seems I'm caught within my own mind, like a bird in a jess, trying to fly from captivity but loving the feeling of being caught. Fear is sadder in truancy than a trope, which declares self-avoidance to understand itself. O what halts a mind's peregrination is that scallion, that pundit of pernickety pretence, that lustful knave whose self-permutation is all well-ordained as an eagle's periwig, that varmint, perception, who would eat his own dogma's quotations to seem as deified as Nero's quondam copycats, who desire no messenger lest his message puts their own aback into the past. Ay, but most traditions would refuse to grieve their greatest mind, yet mine's a-weary of everything within itself that perdition pecks at our brains like nodding hens in a burning church. The copious whispers of self-damnation exude in me like a fistula growing as a weed on the skull. You come here in dominance of the scene, and expect me clone myself like a chitin, feign complicity and give errands to myself that do not wend my ways? One moment you're frightnened as a child in a tempest, the next you coordinate everyone into your idioms like the soldiers of an story bound war. You're a poet waiting for his turn to go mad, like a visitor in heaven. Hamlet's ghost comes crouching near the speeches of Apollo, who has granted us a certain knowledge of the scene, but, as Sybil knows, there is always something else to be understood in the craft of such a God. To maroon my objective leaves me as lonely as a soul in the kalpa of its flesh, jested from God by its own proportion to the life it should've lived. Let's leave a man to his foe and tell him he's a leman . . . I say, a hero needs a villain, like a clown who hams the life of Yorick. The hamartia a man must have to take his own life. O to die a martyr to yourself . . . a New Age hamadryad. There is no deferral in a father's premise that will dissuade his gibbeted words and sweeten his uxorial rose? Tell me, who would Hellenize the Roman's armour and call him loyal? Febrile words cannot belong to self-ravening phrases that would seek out the helminthes' trail for left-behind ambitions. Now is it unruly to wallow in the gaur of succinct realities. If there is a worm in my brain, it matters not what it eats, it matters why it was hungry to commence. If there was ever a mystery that could expound the slavery of my wit, it's the one that you must now become. Be what you will . . . but be not sly as a worm in a doomsday puddle; to understand a role, firstly understand he who plays it . . . how playful do you feel that you've chosen this stage to die on? Like the devil . . . you used my passion against me like a toad in a well. You made me cast my play into the river because you knew it would overshadow this drab presentation of life in toto. This art that you witness is nothing but an argument against the destiny of man, and you hear it like trolls in a wonderland tragedy of angels. And he has befuddled you to your seats like patient gods divining nothing but lies within yourselves. This is only the temporary fossil of a temporary man. It may last a season; but for a book to be a marvel down the ages, it must show mankind the troubles that even a spiritual age cannot disarm, nor dream away the sickness. Show a man what he is, he'll never gorge another lie, nor brook another rote in his turn, nor do anything that could make away with his bliss. If you are to be a thespian, tell them things they would not have thought without you. I was once a dullard of language myself, whose motive grew on his duplicity, like thistles on the gardener's brain. How do I partake it? I'll par the noble sorrow and take away its form to imagine it as a counterfeit, a beauty that riles forth all the traditions of deceit. Infinity on high . . . you <u>will</u> remember me. And sapience, like a dying old man, reminds me I am to the skull with knowledge, yet with an unschooled heart a man concedes his victuals of time to be wary of any loss that wages against the memory of his sins, to be as exact in guilt as a portion of lust weighed against the desires of the lecher, or a golden rhapsody spoken like a vision to the blind. For in each of us there is a daemon who awaits our sanction, he follows us to the wake of simple pleasures, and feeds upon the fissures like an insatiable weed, a word that struggles to remain unbothered by its meaning, like a man unconvinced of his soul. If I am to indulge in this the least of my own acumen, like an explorer defining the limits of the land by his own doubt, then the impetigo has also reached my oblivion. And so, in this ailing lust of convocation, I lead astray the dying, that the living might never know what is to become of them. For a man and his disaster, himself oblivious of the means, goes to his grave unfathomed of the deed that damns him, that brings him to the osmosis of an undraped instinct, which to him is nothing more than lust, or a weathered sense of self, but to God is the difference between a man and a beast. Though neither bodes for paradise, at least a man needs not attend to the goings of a beast in constant famine, to resolve the instinct of his doing and stanch the import of his breath, lest it becomes a disease of insight and tills from him the language of deceit, the air of presumption, the contagion of shame, the malarkey of dementia and, alas, the everlasting idleness of a man in the everlasting desert of himself. God's consciousness is unattainable to Man: what paradise shall we have if it is sought in another man's Perdition? Do you ambuscade your own will? Think like a saint, and so begins the sainthood, like a window stained by its own pitch of execution, whose censure is not left without resolve, though the truth manumits its own epilogue. God proffers the mind with a cup of light, and a flagon of Christ's blood. So call yourself enlightened, like ready fireflies at Jesus's tomb, who dragoon a fear from the urchin's silence, where the spirit's hour descends into the heart withal. Words would sully the observance but never what defines him as paladins of passion, like a ghost, shapeless though shape pronounces him to the world like an orb. Give it to the linctus of your Duchess coven. The plebeian shores are drenched in Papago's blood. Man is in dire need of poriferan reproof, like a beetroot in the garden of Eden. O God, to me this world is an impossible trial of the will; it is a cold vengeance waiting to quicken up the winds into our lungs. I am weary of this flesh, it reminds me incessantly that I am but an augur made spendthrift by doubt, by fear, by revelations that he himself would never speak, with no knowledge of the life that never ceases to inquire the abyss where no life enters. Amen.